Travel To...
REAL CASTLES
AROUND THE WORLD

Kaitlyn Duling

Before Reading: *Building Background Knowledge and Vocabulary*

Building background knowledge can help children process new information and build upon what they already know. Before reading a book, it is important to tap into what children already know about the topic. This will help them develop their vocabulary and increase their reading comprehension.

Questions and Activities to Build Background Knowledge:

1. Look at the front cover of the book and read the title. What do you think this book will be about?
2. What do you already know about this topic?
3. Take a book walk and skim the pages. Look at the table of contents, photographs, captions, and bold words. Did these text features give you any information or predictions about what you will read in this book?

Vocabulary: *Vocabulary Is Key to Reading Comprehension*

Use the following directions to prompt a conversation about each word:

- Read the vocabulary words.
- What comes to mind when you see each word?
- What do you think each word means?

Vocabulary Words:
- abbey
- archaeology
- arrowslits
- citadel
- colony
- dungeon
- medieval
- moat
- monarchs
- pilgrimage
- residence
- turrets

During Reading: *Reading for Meaning and Understanding*

To achieve deep comprehension of a book, children are encouraged to use close reading strategies. During reading, it is important to have children stop and make connections. These connections result in deeper analysis and understanding of a book.

Close Reading a Text

During reading, have children stop and talk about the following:

- Any confusing parts
- Any unknown words
- Text to text, text to self, text to world connections
- The main idea in each chapter or heading

These strategies will help children learn to analyze the text more thoroughly as they read.

When you are finished reading this book, turn to page 46 for **Text-Dependent Questions** and an **Extension Activity**.

TABLE of CONTENTS

REAL CASTLES

AROUND THE WORLD

Picture a castle in your mind. What do you see? Perhaps a mighty fortress with a drawbridge, or a palace with towers that seem to touch the sky. These buildings don't just live in our fairy tales and imaginations. *Real* castles dot the globe, from Europe's **medieval** walls to Japan's great palaces, and everywhere in between. In fact, castles can be found on nearly every continent!

For hundreds of years, these enchanting structures have been built with different residents in mind. Some were—and still are—elaborate homes for royalty. Others were designed to keep enemies out. Still others were monasteries or showpieces for colonial powers.

Whether citadel, chateau, court, or keep, castles have captured our collective imagination. Let's go! It's time to travel to . . . real castles around the world.

Château de Chenonceau, France

Neuschwanstein Castle,
Germany
Palace of Versailles,
France
Castle of the Moors,
Portugal

DREAMING

OF CASTLES

NEUSCHWANSTEIN CASTLE

SCHWANGAU, GERMANY

Does this castle look familiar? Walt Disney used Neuschwanstein Castle as his inspiration for Sleeping Beauty's castle at Disneyland.

King Ludwig II designed the **residence** for ultimate privacy. It is hidden amidst the forests of the Bavarian Alps.

Sleeping Beauty Castle, Disneyland

Construction began in 1868. Then, in June 1886, the King's body was found in a lake. To this day, his death remains mysterious. Of the 200 rooms he had planned for the castle, only 14 were completed. Each year, more than one million visitors tour those rooms, take in the beautiful views, and explore the mysteries of Neuschwanstein.

FACT OR FICTION?

Was Bran Castle in Romania home to a real vampire? Probably not. But author Bram Stoker may have used it as inspiration for Dracula's Castle. It is the only castle in the Transylvania region that fits Stoker's description: ". . . on the very edge of a terrific precipice . . . with occasionally a deep rift where there is a chasm [with] silver threads where the rivers wind in deep gorges through the forests."

EDINBURGH CASTLE

EDINBURGH, SCOTLAND

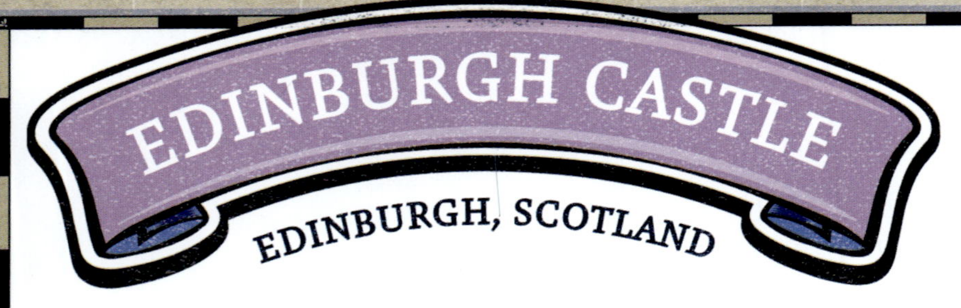

Walking up to Castle Rock in Edinburgh, Scotland, can feel like flying into a magical world of witches and wizards—and like stepping way, way back in time! This site has been occupied since 850 BCE. The castle itself, which bears a striking resemblance to a certain wizard school, was built in 1103. Some say Edinburgh may have inspired some scenes and themes from the Harry Potter book series.

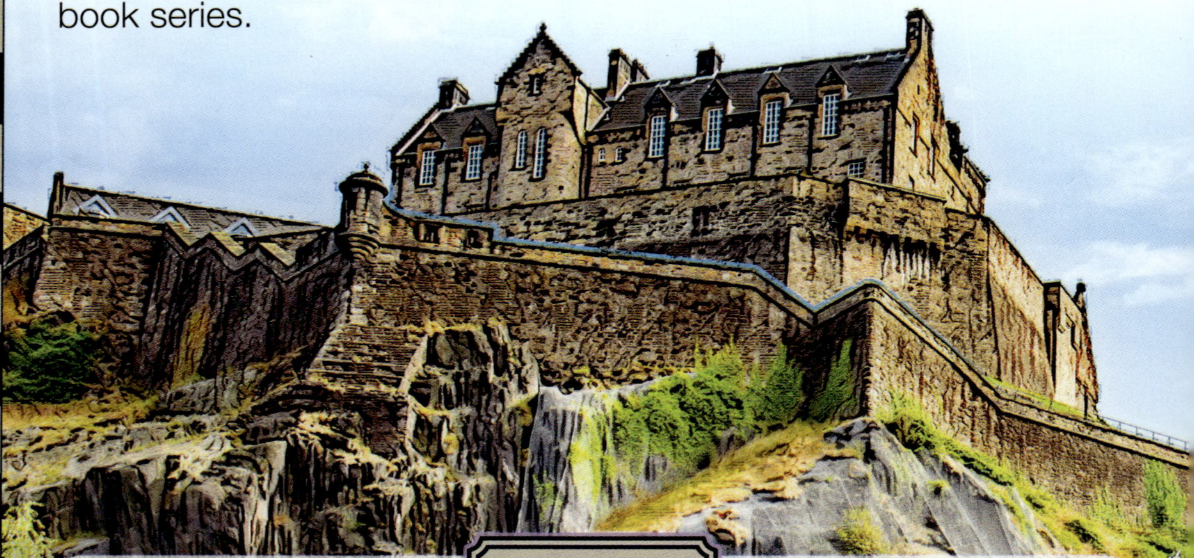

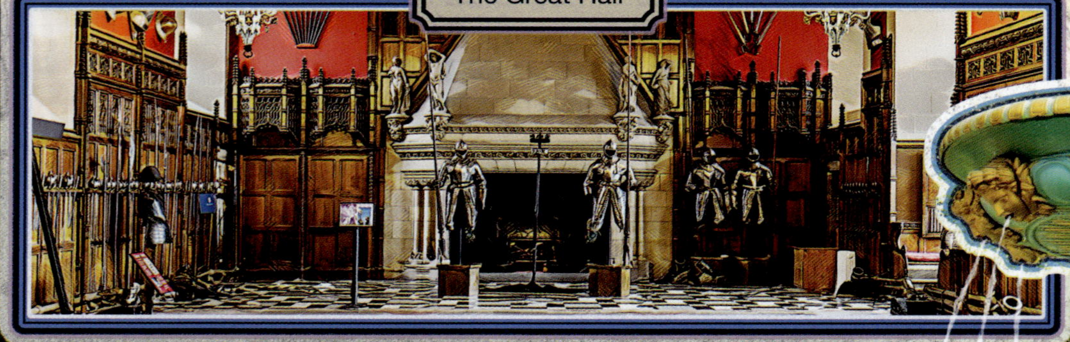

The Great Hall

Through the centuries, Edinburgh Castle has been used as a royal residence, a military base, and even a prison.

The last king to live here was Charles I, in 1633. Travelers now flock to the castle to peek at the Great Hall, the coronation throne, and Mons Meg, a giant 15th-century cannon.

STAR STRONGHOLD

For most of its 900-year history, Alnwick Castle in Northumberland, England, was a family home—and a formidable fortress. Recently, though, it has taken a starring role in more than 40 movies and TV shows, including Downton Abbey, Transformers: The Last Knight, Star Trek: The Next Generation, Westworld, and many more.

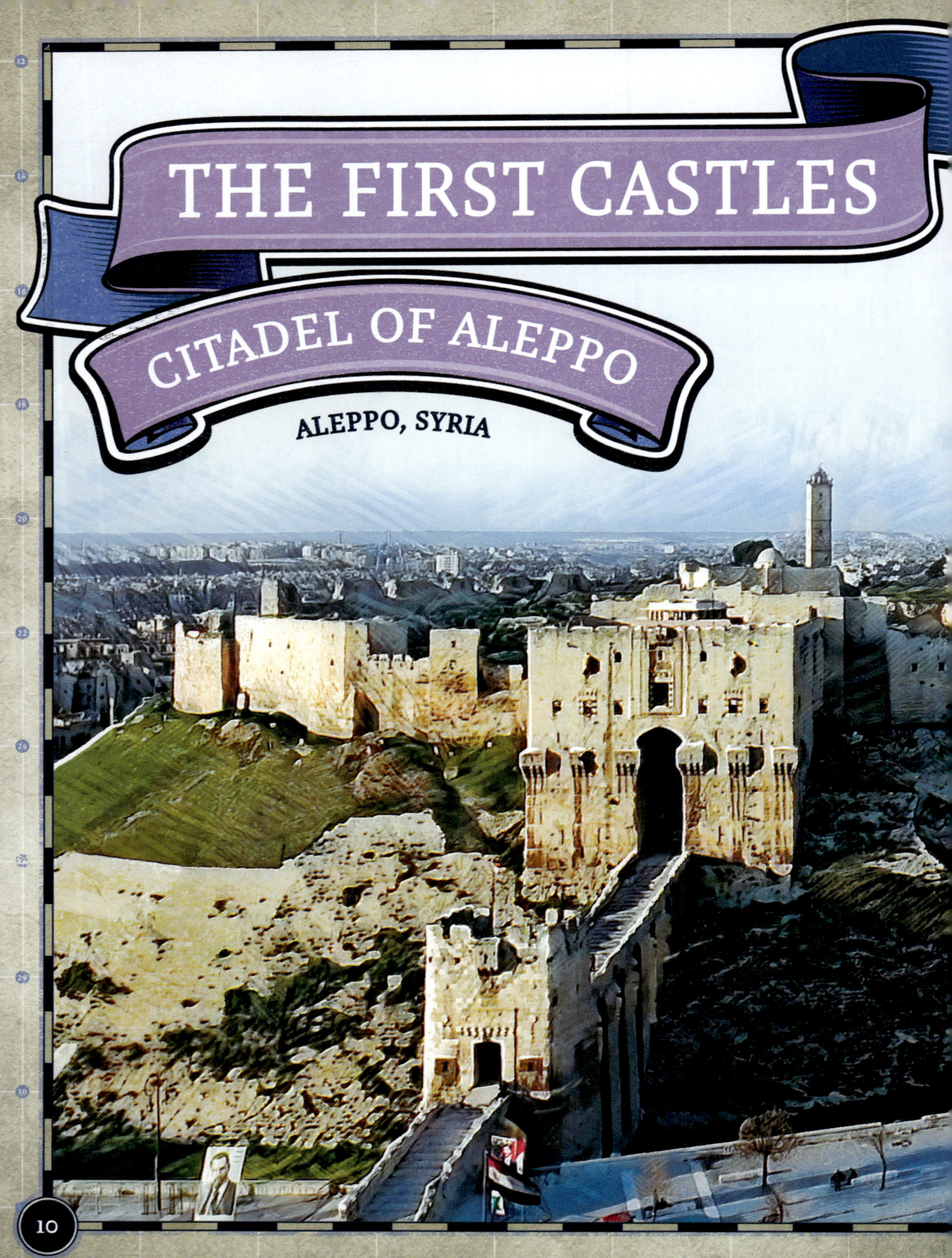

THE FIRST CASTLES

CITADEL OF ALEPPO

ALEPPO, SYRIA

The term ***citadel*** means "little city." This massive, oval-shaped fortress has, over many centuries, earned that name. Its many buildings, fortified walls, and towering gateways combine military might with beautiful Islamic architecture. The citadel contains a royal palace complex, mosques (Islamic places of worship), *madrasas* (schools), public baths, and much more.

Aleppo is one of the oldest cities in the world. Construction on the hill is said to have begun as early as the third century BCE. Secret underground passageways may have linked the citadel to the city outside its walls.

GREAT ZIMBABWE
SOUTHEASTERN ZIMBABWE

Tall granite towers. Earthen mounds and mud-brick structures. The ruins of a palace. All encircled by a massive, curving stone wall. This is all that remains of Great Zimbabwe, a culture of immense wealth and architectural skill that thrived from the 11th to the 15th century CE.

Much of Great Zimbabwe and its people are still a mystery, though the sophisticated stone ruins have intrigued travelers and scholars for centuries. Stone birds perch on the outer walls; they are thought to be sacred to the Shona people. Today, the birds are featured on the flag of the Republic of Zimbabwe.

WINDSOR CASTLE

WINDSOR, ENGLAND

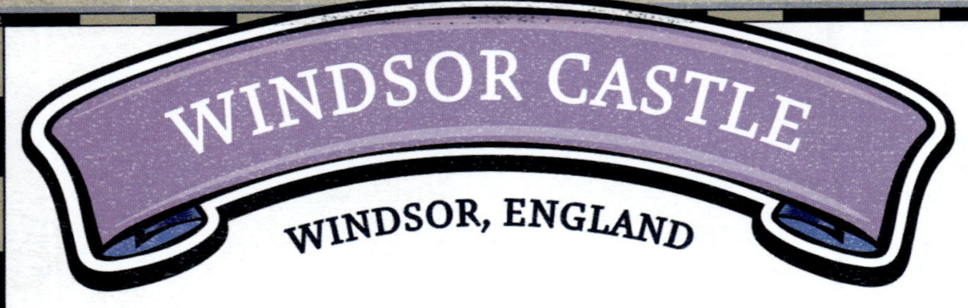

Since around 1070, Windsor Castle has been built, expanded, redecorated, and reimagined by the British royal family. Over the centuries, more than 40 **monarchs** have called the castle home. What started as a wooden fortress was turned to stone by King Henry II. King George IV chose much of the furniture.

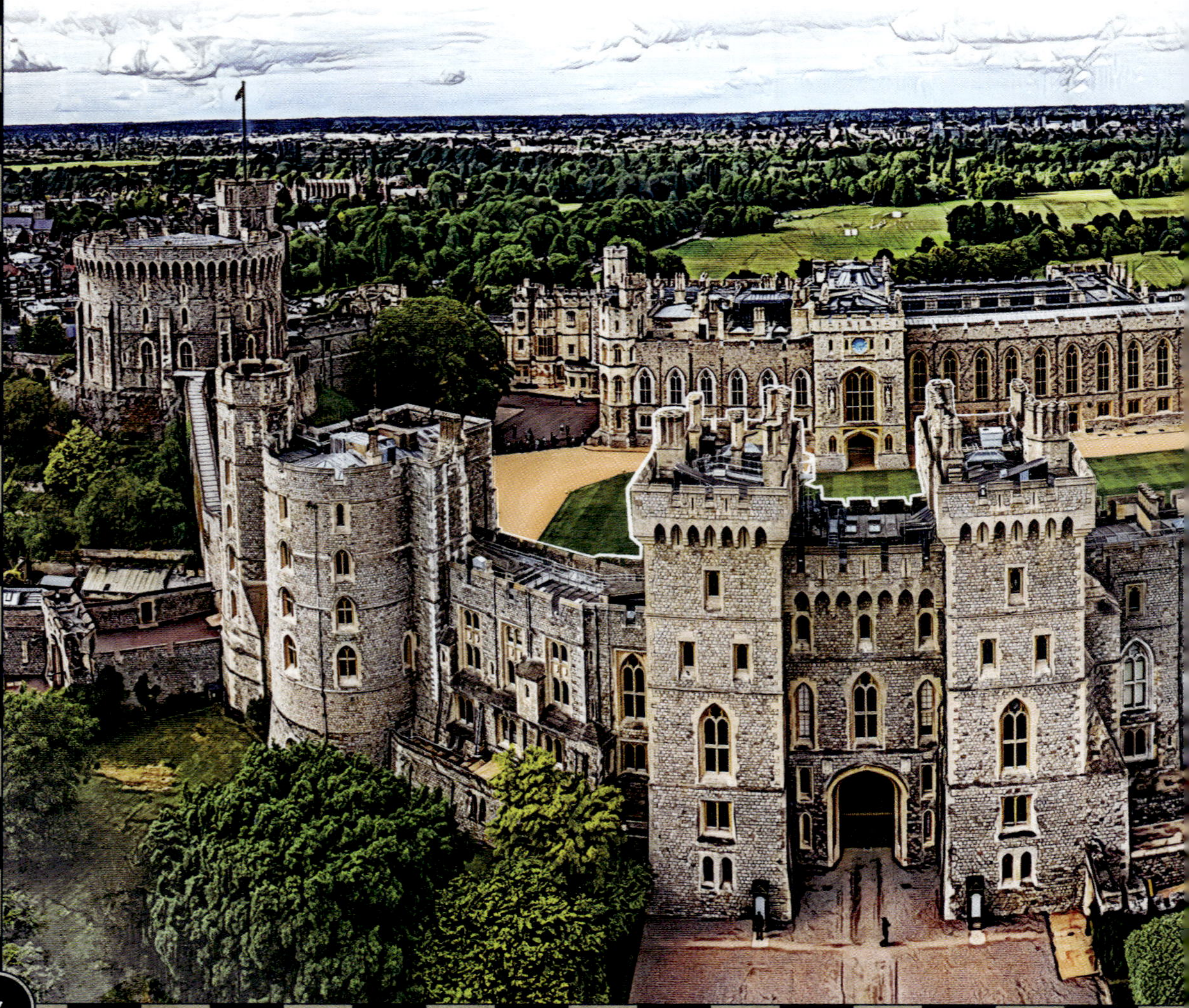

Windsor is the oldest and largest inhabited castle on Earth. Around 150 staff live on the property year-round, which is both a home and a venue for ceremonies. Eleven monarchs are buried at Windsor Castle. But over 25 ghosts are said to haunt the property. Who could they be? To meet them, you'll have to visit!

FAST FACTS ABOUT WINDSOR CASTLE

- *The castle was built to overlook the River Thames and the Windsor Forest, which was a popular hunting ground.*

- *In 1992, a fire damaged more than 100 rooms. It took 15 hours to put out.*

- *The clocks in the castle's Great Kitchen are set five minutes fast to ensure the monarch's food is never late.*

HIMEJI CASTLE

HIMEJI, JAPAN

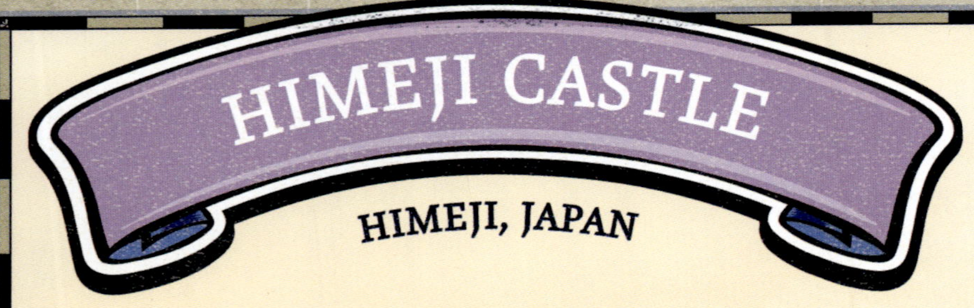

Over time, many castles around the world have been destroyed by war, fire, or earthquakes. But not Himeji Castle. This Japanese fortress, built around 1609, is full of defensive features. It was built to last.

Himeji has a maze of passageways and gates meant to confuse invaders, as well as specially built windows from which stones can be dropped on approaching armies. In all, this massive castle complex has more than 80 buildings connected by winding paths. It's surrounded by a **moat**—a popular defensive feature of castles built during the Middle Ages.

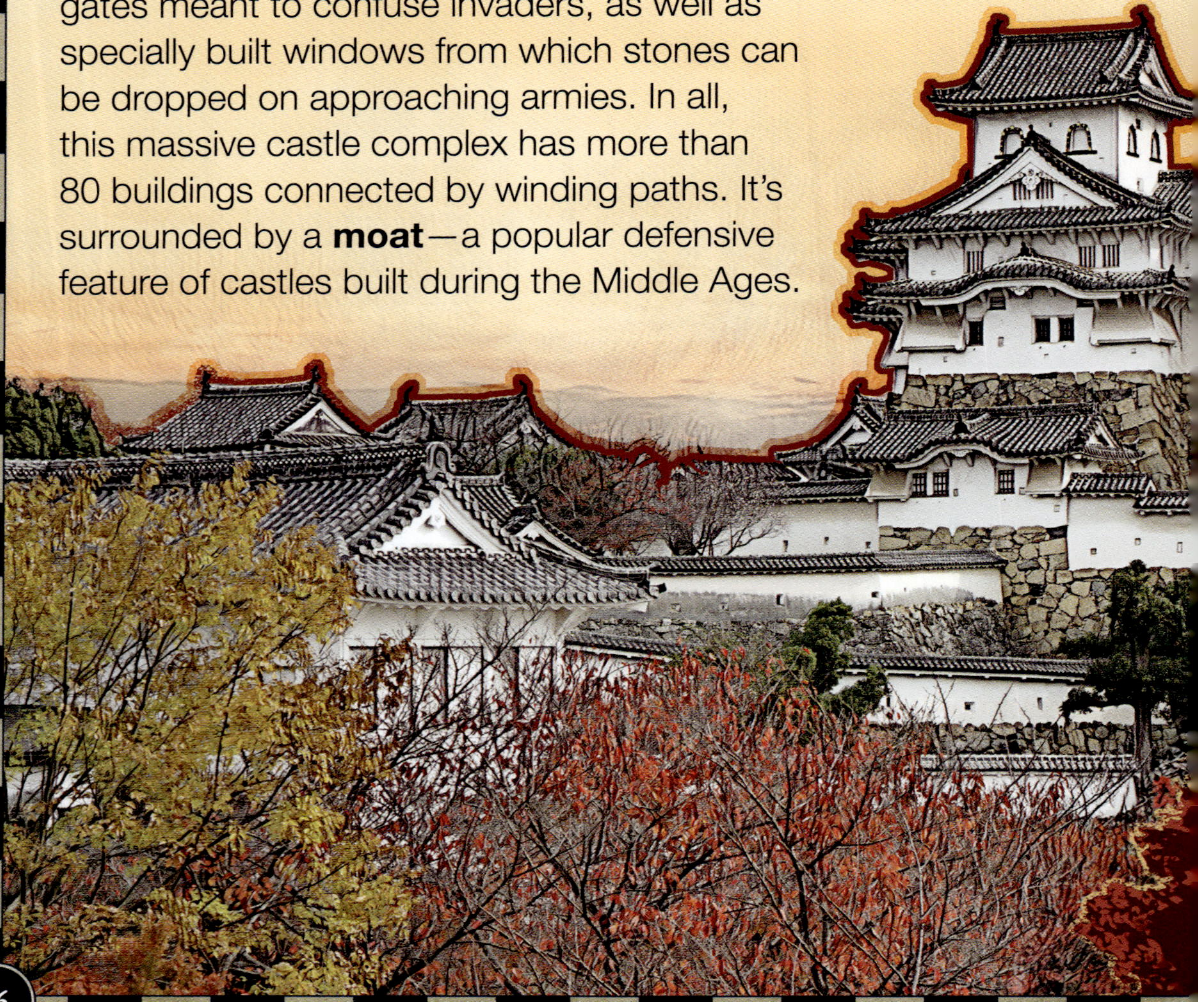

MATSUMOTO'S MOAT

- - - - - - - - - - - - - - - - - -

Matsumoto Castle in Japan, also known as Crow Castle due to its black exterior, has a triple moat system. Along the outer moat are hundreds of cherry trees that burst into bloom every spring. Delicate and defensive— this castle is both!

- - - - - - - - - - - - - - - - - -

Himeji is one of the oldest and most-visited castles in Japan. Its white-plastered buildings, topped with tiled roofs that look like bird's wings, earned it the nickname White Heron Castle.

Perched on a vertical cliff face, Predjama Castle is the largest cave castle in the world! In the 15th century, it was also the perfect hiding spot for Erasmus of Lueg, a legendary knight who was said to have been a thief who gave away the items he stole.

Whenever he was under siege, Erasmus used a secret passage to enter and exit the castle. When enemies tried to starve him, Erasmus received food through the extensive cave system under the castle. And, according to legend, the knight met his demise when a cannonball was strategically fired . . . at the castle's restroom.

The castle's caves are now home to a bat colony. Adventurous visitors can tour them, as well as the dank **dungeon** and several re-created interior rooms.

QASR KHARANA

AMMAN, JORDAN

Here, in the far reaches of the treeless, vast Jordanian desert, miles from the nearest city, is Qasr Kharana: a desert castle. It is just one of many ancient desert palaces in present-day Jordan.

According to historians, this desert castle probably dates back to before 710 CE. Its thick, imposing walls nearly form a square. Inside, visitors can walk in the courtyard and peer into 60 small rooms.

Historians aren't entirely sure why Qasr Kharana was built. It doesn't appear to be a defensive fort. The solid towers couldn't be used by armed soldiers. And it would be impossible to fire through the openings that look like **arrowslits** in the castle's walls; they are too narrow. Some historians speculate that the structure was used as a meeting place.

Arrowslits

Entrance to
Qasr Kharana

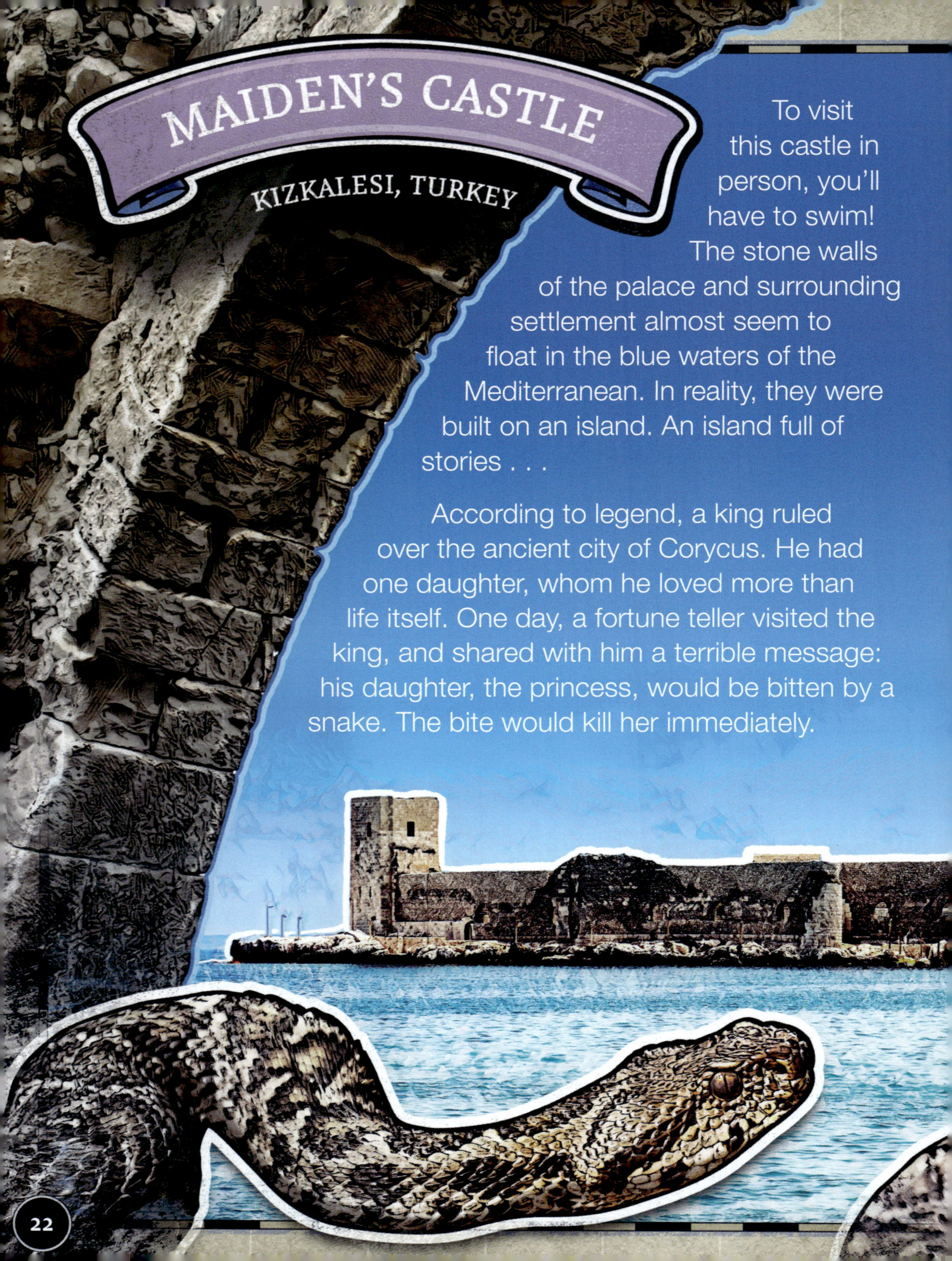

To visit this castle in person, you'll have to swim! The stone walls of the palace and surrounding settlement almost seem to float in the blue waters of the Mediterranean. In reality, they were built on an island. An island full of stories . . .

According to legend, a king ruled over the ancient city of Corycus. He had one daughter, whom he loved more than life itself. One day, a fortune teller visited the king, and shared with him a terrible message: his daughter, the princess, would be bitten by a snake. The bite would kill her immediately.

The king was distraught and determined to save the princess. So, believing snakes could not swim, he built a castle on an island in the middle of the sea, and locked her inside. All was well until one day when the princess requested some grapes for lunch. A basket was sent over. It was full of grapes—and a snake. The fortune teller's vision came true, and now, only the castle remains.

Byzantine art

ANOTHER STORY

Kizkalesi means "Maiden's Castle," and refers to the legend of the king and princess. But according to historians, the castle was likely built by the Byzantines sometime around 1099 CE.

MONT-SAINT-MICHEL

NORMANDY, FRANCE

This castle celebrated its 1,000th birthday in 2023. Rising out of a tidal island in Normandy, the Mont-Saint-Michel is one of the most-visited sites in France. This is thanks to its beauty—and its backstory.

According to long-held legends, the Archangel Michael appeared to a French bishop in 708 CE and instructed him to build a church on some far-off rocks in the bay. Since then, the island's castle—really a Benedictine **abbey**—has been an active **pilgrimage** site.

Those who do visit must leave their cars on the mainland. The Mont-Saint-Michel is only accessible on foot, by shuttle bus, or by horse-drawn carriage.

Statue of Saint Michael

TROSKY CASTLE, CZECH REPUBLIC

To capture Trosky Castle, enemies would need to venture to the top of a volcanic mountain! To this day, it has never been conquered by a military.

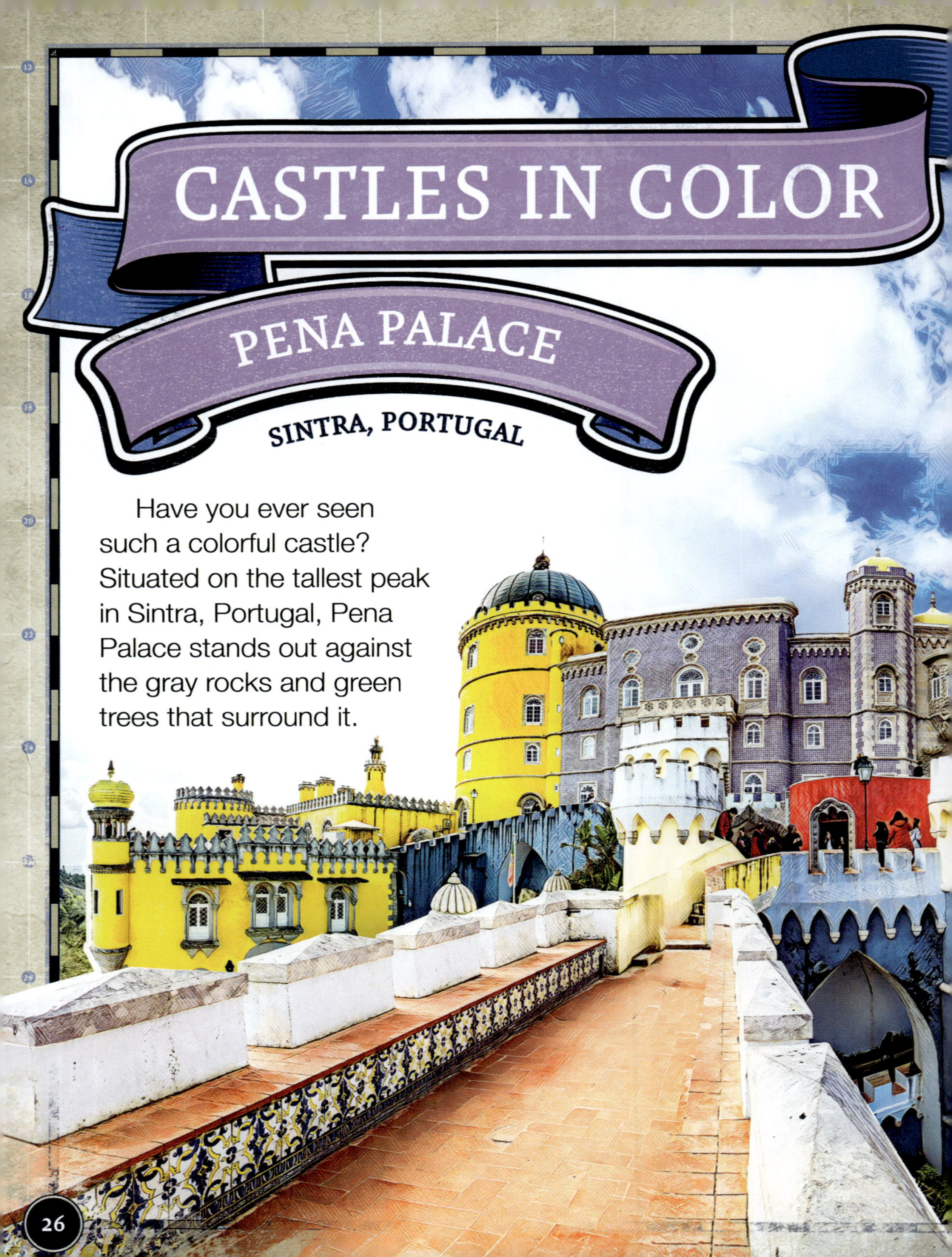

CASTLES IN COLOR

PENA PALACE

SINTRA, PORTUGAL

Have you ever seen such a colorful castle? Situated on the tallest peak in Sintra, Portugal, Pena Palace stands out against the gray rocks and green trees that surround it.

The site of the palace has been a place of pilgrimage since the Middle Ages. In the 1500s, a monastery was built, and then in 1842, King Ferdinand II began constructing a grand residence. Today, the former monastery buildings are painted red, while the New Palace—inspired by the castles of Bavaria—is bright yellow.

The complex is intricately designed, with towers and terraces at several different levels. Around the castle, King Ferdinand built the Park of Pena, which he filled with exotic plants and winding paths.

CRIMSON CASTLE

Since the late 1300s, Shuri Castle in Japan has been built, rebuilt, and rebuilt again! It was destroyed during the Battle of Okinawa in 1945 and then by fire in 2019. Despite the damage, it has retained its bright red hue. The red roof tiles, made of mudstone, help keep the inside of the structure cool, even under the hot Okinawa sun.

KELBURN CASTLE

NORTH AYRSHIRE, SCOTLAND

Kelburn Castle, home to the Earl of Glasgow, is one of the oldest castles in Scotland. Parts of the structure date to the 13th century. But the art on its walls is decidedly contemporary!

In 2007, Lord Glasgow invited four Brazilian graffiti artists to paint a portion of this historic rural castle. For one month, they lived together inside the castle, turning its walls and its **turrets** into a work of art. At the time, some community members were angry about the art. They thought the colorful, vibrant images had no place in Kelburn's rural landscape. Others thought the graffiti made a strong artistic statement. They loved the castle's new, entirely unique look.

Kelburn, now known as Scotland's "graffiti castle," is an 800-year-old structure that continues to make history—one colorful wall at a time.

TURRETS EXPLAINED

- - - - - - - - - - - - - - - - - -

Castle turrets aren't just beautiful. In medieval times, they served an important defensive purpose! Unlike square towers, round turrets don't have any corners or flat surfaces, both of which can be weak points during an attack. Additionally, some believe turrets allowed soldiers a better view of attackers.

- - - - - - - - - - - - - - - - - -

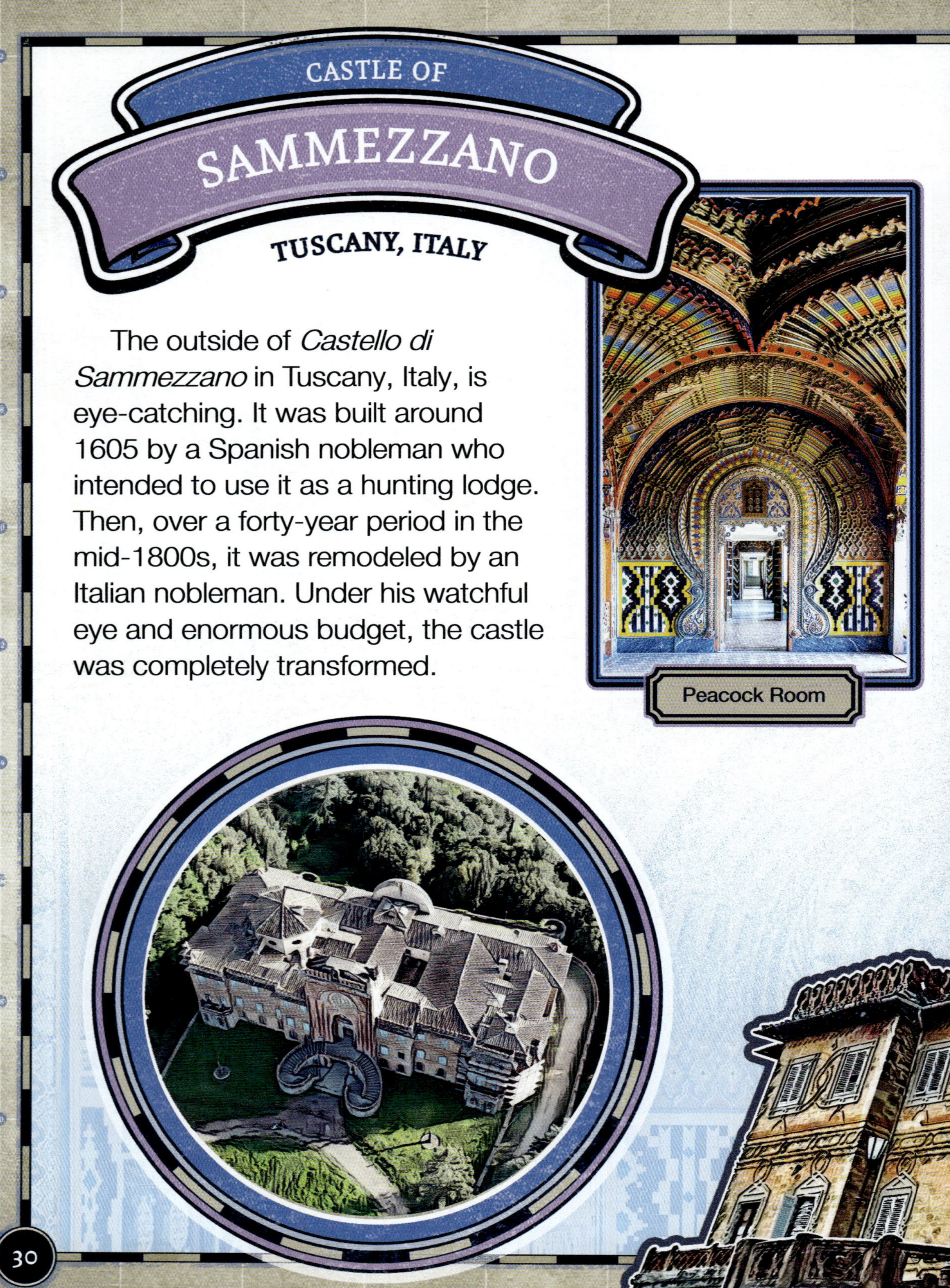

CASTLE OF SAMMEZZANO

TUSCANY, ITALY

The outside of *Castello di Sammezzano* in Tuscany, Italy, is eye-catching. It was built around 1605 by a Spanish nobleman who intended to use it as a hunting lodge. Then, over a forty-year period in the mid-1800s, it was remodeled by an Italian nobleman. Under his watchful eye and enormous budget, the castle was completely transformed.

Peacock Room

To see the castle's most captivating colors and patterns, you've got to go inside. There are 365 rooms—one for every day of the year. Each has its own name and unique style pulled from Moorish, Byzantine, Indian, and Chinese influences. There's the mosaic-tiled White Room, the brightly colored Peacock Room, and the dazzling Room of the Mirrors. Over the centuries, the castle has been used as a residence, a hotel, and even a bar. These days, unfortunately, it remains closed to the public.
Curious travelers hope one day
the doors will open again.

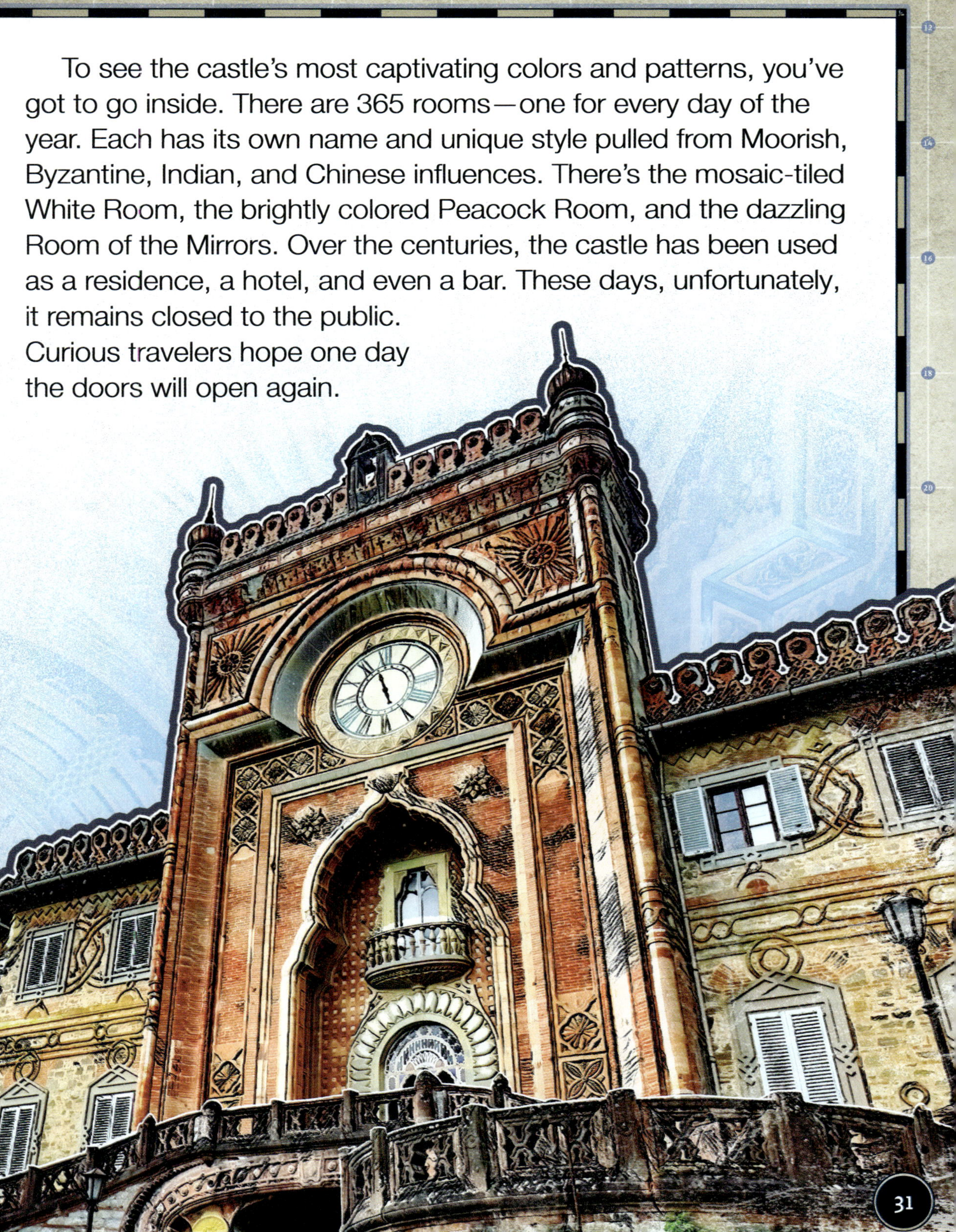

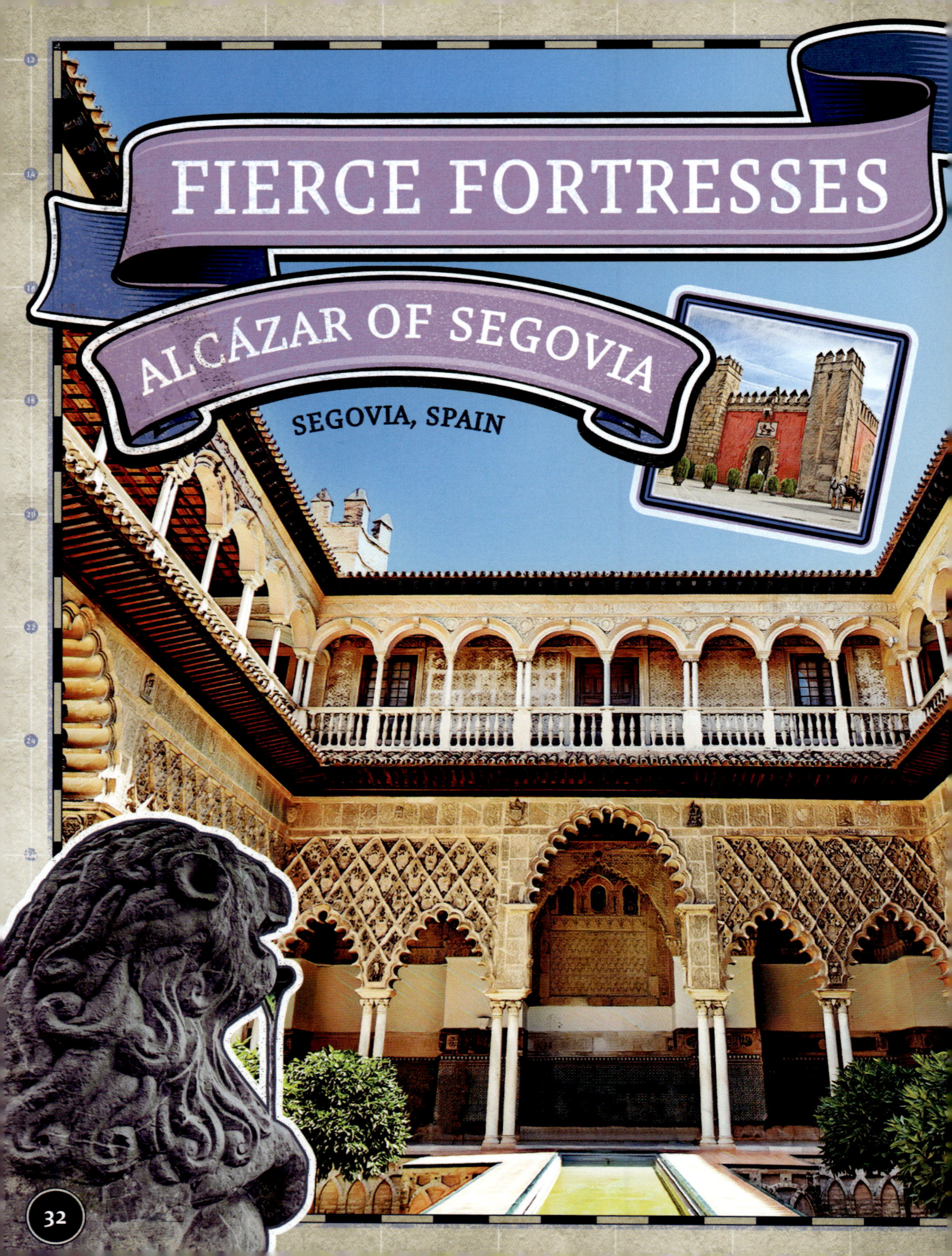

FIERCE FORTRESSES
ALCÁZAR OF SEGOVIA
SEGOVIA, SPAIN

It may look like a fairy tale, but this castle was built as a defensive fortress, high up on a massive rock. About an hour and a half outside of Madrid, Spain, visitors to Alcázar can step back in time—to at least the 12th century, when the earliest-known records of the castle were made. Its location offered an ideal position from which to defend against attacks. A deep moat, tall towers, and thick stone walls made it nearly impenetrable.

Over the centuries, the castle has been rebuilt, renovated, and reimagined again and again. It has housed royalty, served as a state prison, been home to a military college, and was eventually transformed into a museum.

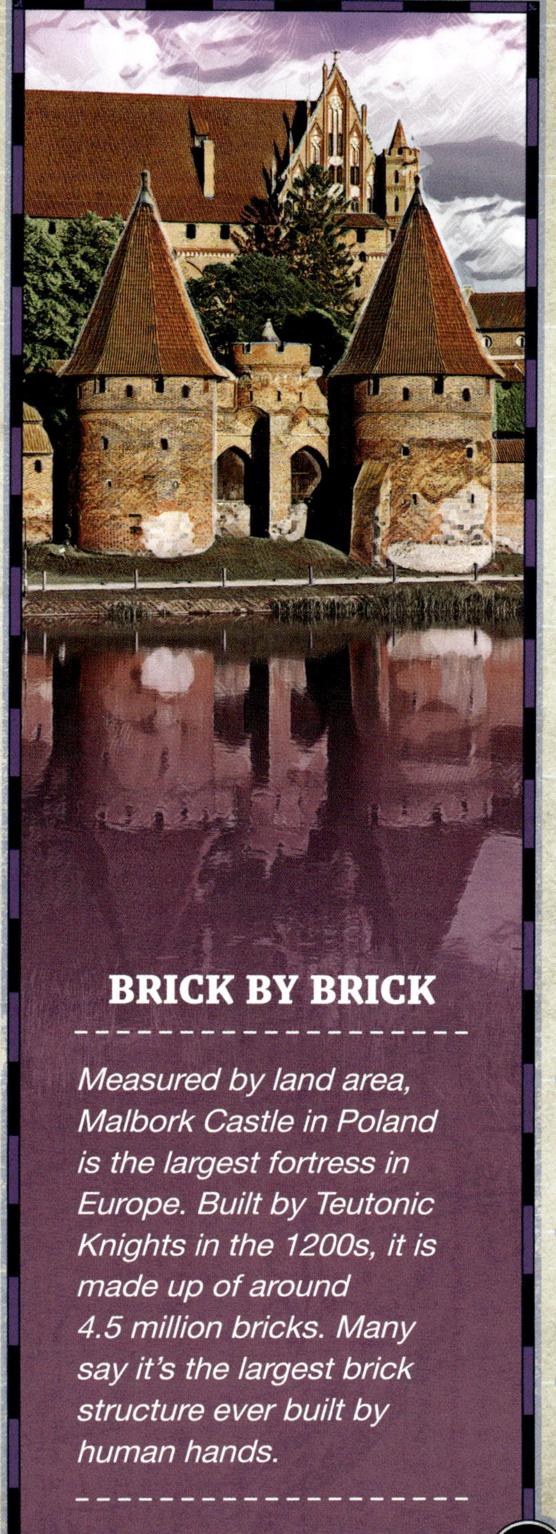

BRICK BY BRICK

Measured by land area, Malbork Castle in Poland is the largest fortress in Europe. Built by Teutonic Knights in the 1200s, it is made up of around 4.5 million bricks. Many say it's the largest brick structure ever built by human hands.

CHITTORGARH

RAJASTHAN, INDIA

Visiting some historic fortresses feels like taking a peek directly into the past. That's because they have been carefully preserved over hundreds and even thousands of years. This fortress, known as Chittor or Chittorgarh, is one of the largest in all of India. Parts of the fort date back to at least the 8th century.

One of many "hill forts" in the region, Chittorgarh sits atop a nearly 196-foot-tall (180-meters-tall) hill. More than eight miles (13 kilometers) of stone walls surround a castle complex made up of palaces, temples, and towers.

Over its long history, the site has been attacked, seized, and partially destroyed many times over. The fort remains popular with visitors, who travel to tour the grounds, visit its museum, and take part in the many festivals and fairs held there all year round.

Kirti Stambha
(Tower of Fame)

GAUMUKH RESERVOIR

One of the most visited and most sacred places inside Chittorgarh is Gaumukh Reservoir. Water flows into the tank via a natural spring emerging from an opening in the rocks shaped like a cow's mouth. Gaumukh means "cow's mouth."

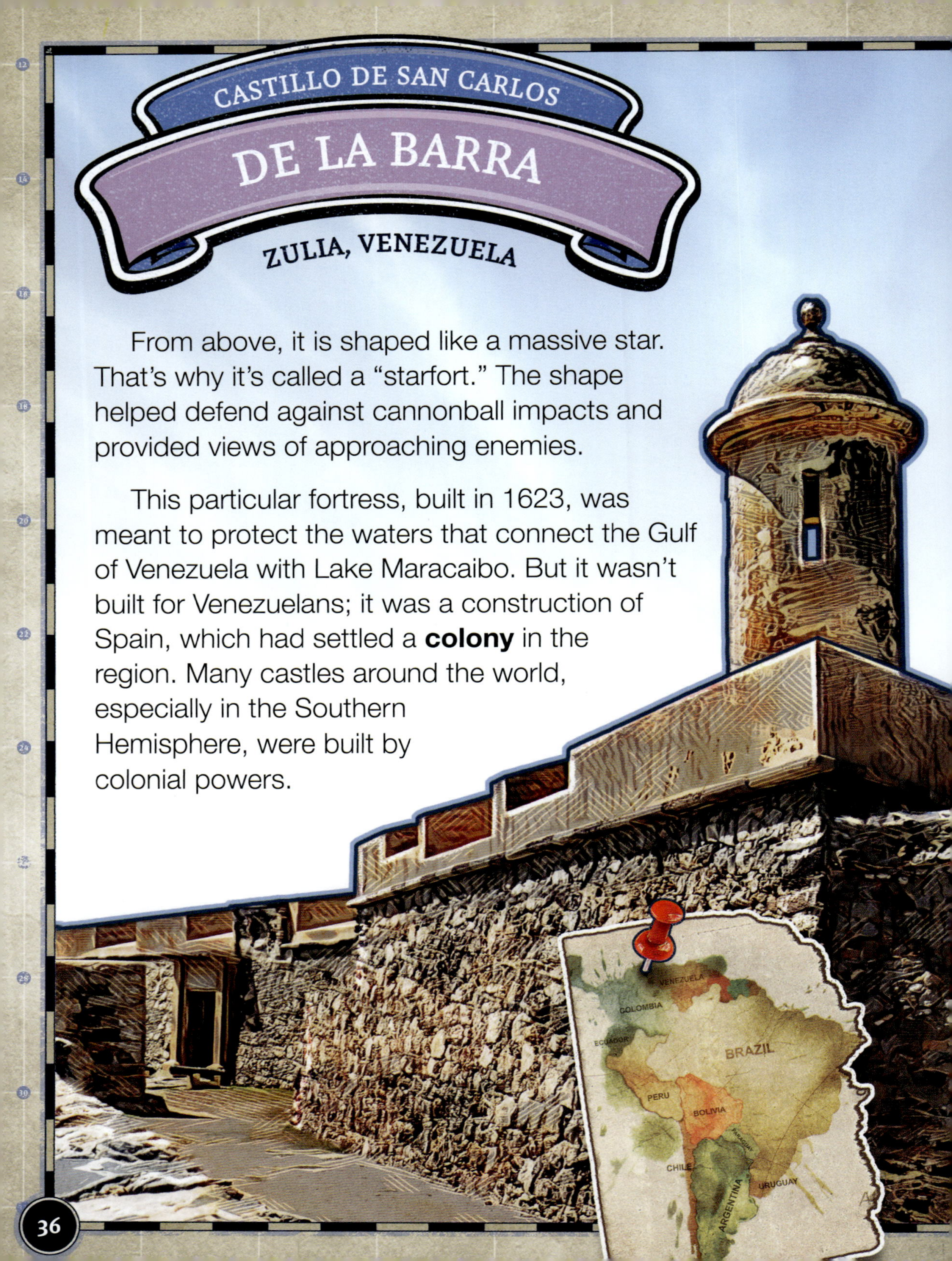

From above, it is shaped like a massive star. That's why it's called a "starfort." The shape helped defend against cannonball impacts and provided views of approaching enemies.

This particular fortress, built in 1623, was meant to protect the waters that connect the Gulf of Venezuela with Lake Maracaibo. But it wasn't built for Venezuelans; it was a construction of Spain, which had settled a **colony** in the region. Many castles around the world, especially in the Southern Hemisphere, were built by colonial powers.

They did this to protect themselves, to demonstrate power, and to house their leaders.

Castillo de San Carlos de la Barra is one of these colonial fortifications. When it was built, the Spanish hoped they could protect their colony from pirates. After Venezuela achieved independence from Spain in 1819, the fort continued to be used as a defensive structure. In the early 1900s, it withstood bombardments from German warships, and was later used as a prison.

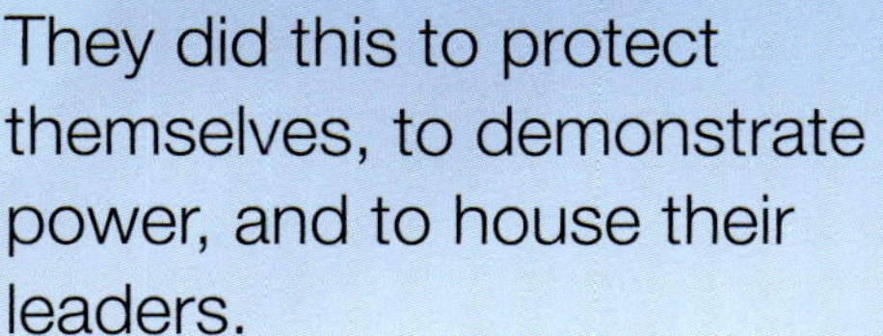

CASTILLO SAN FELIPE DE BARAJAS, COLOMBIA

This fortress—one of the largest colonial forts in the Americas—was built by enslaved Africans forced to work under the Spanish colonial government in 1536. Some consider the complex, which features tunnels, walls, and a grand entrance, to be the single most formidable example of Spanish military architecture built to date.

KENTUCKY CASTLE

KENTUCKY, UNITED STATES

If you travel around the United States, you aren't likely to encounter many medieval-style castles. Why not? The United States was founded centuries after castles had peaked in popularity as royal residences—and long after heavy cannons were introduced, which was a major blow to most castles' defensive capabilities.

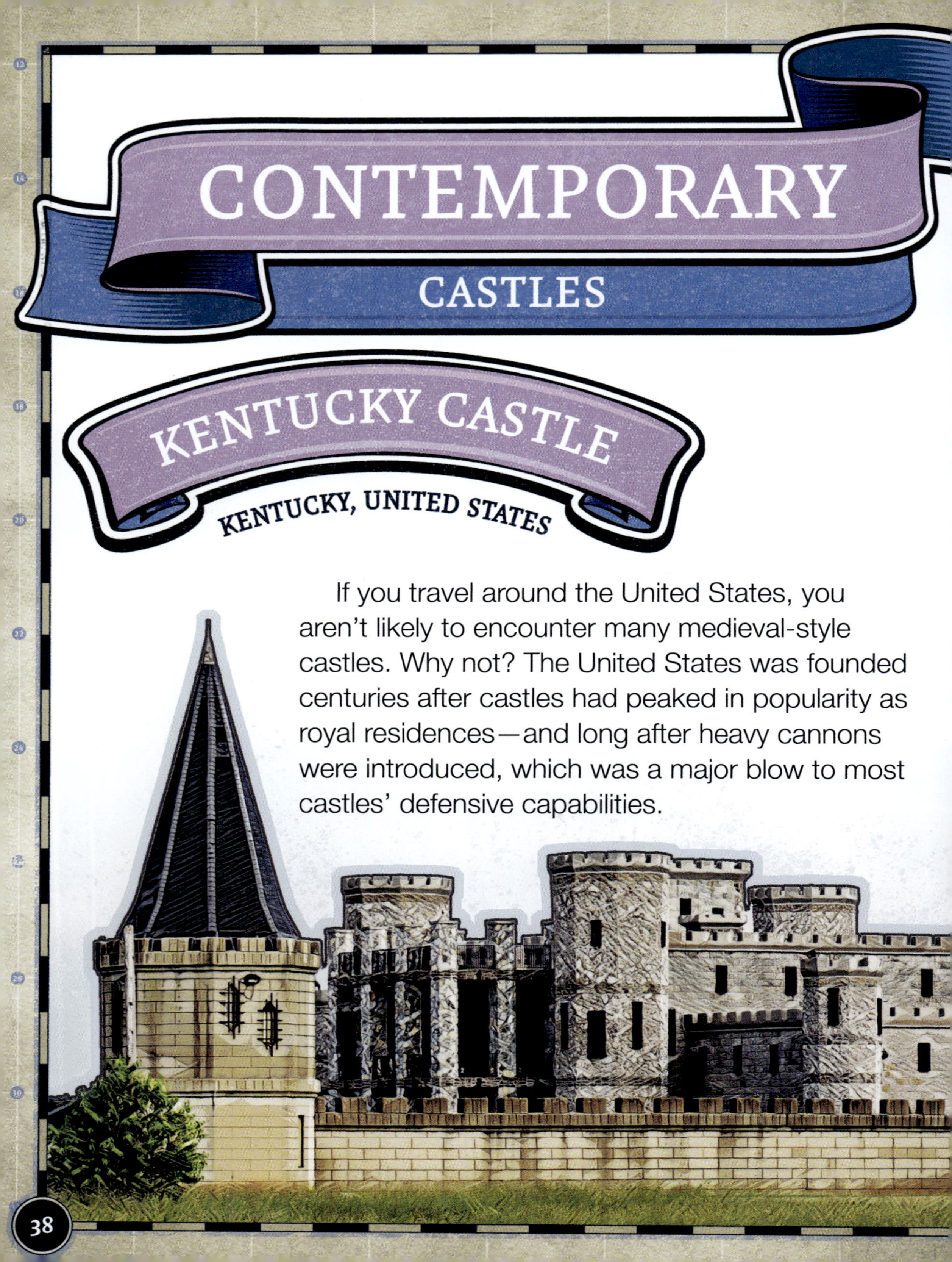

Still, the States are home to plenty of palaces and other structures that could be called castles, even if they are a little . . . unique.

Kentucky Castle, for example, was never a defensive fort. It was never home to royalty. And it definitely wasn't built during the medieval period. In fact, construction on the building, which was used as a private home for many years, began in 1969. After a sale, fire, and a major reconstruction effort, Kentucky Castle was turned into a luxury hotel, restaurant, and event venue. Visitors to this contemporary castle can play on a basketball court, visit a spa, and even spend the night in a luxury suite in one of the castle's four turrets.

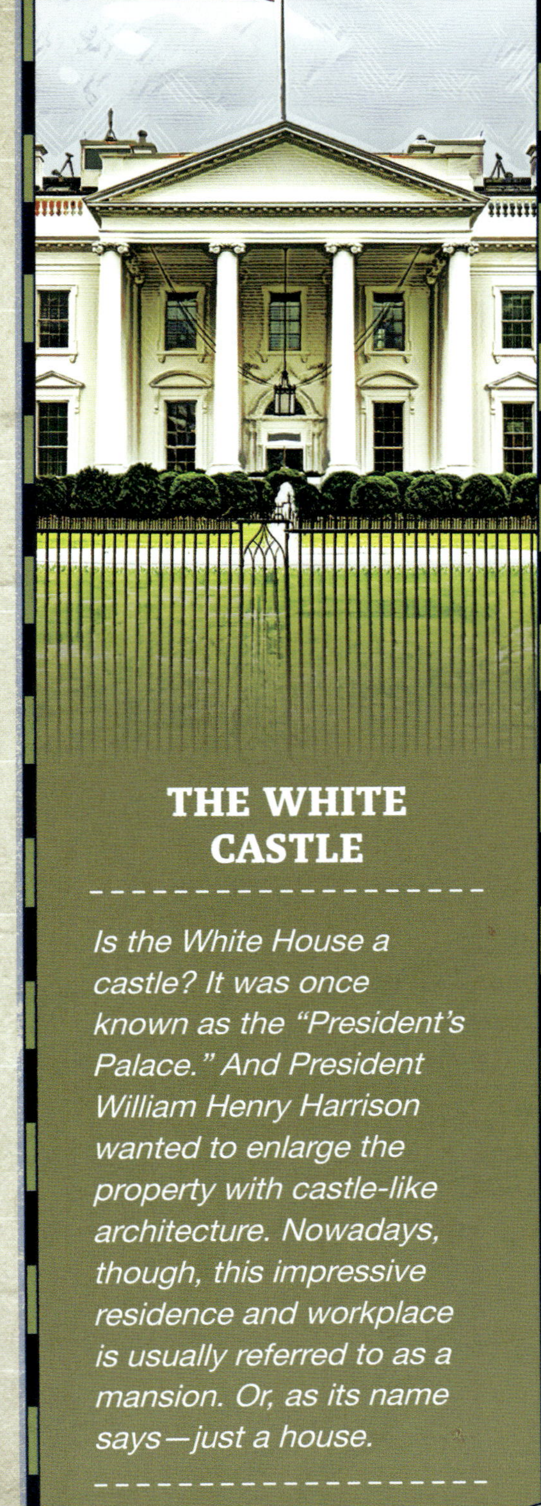

THE WHITE CASTLE

Is the White House a castle? It was once known as the "President's Palace." And President William Henry Harrison wanted to enlarge the property with castle-like architecture. Nowadays, though, this impressive residence and workplace is usually referred to as a mansion. Or, as its name says—just a house.

GUÉDELON CASTLE

TREIGNY, FRANCE

This *looks* like a medieval castle. But construction started in 1997! A team of master builders imagined Guédelon Castle as an experimental **archaeology** project. They wanted to discover the past by constructing a castle in the present. They made a plan, found an abandoned quarry, and got to work.

The castle's designs were modeled after real 13th-century structures. It is being built entirely with handmade materials. The site, which has become a major tourist attraction and an educational center, employs blacksmiths, rope-makers, stonemasons, and more. The workers wear clothing that would be appropriate for the time period, and transport materials using horse-drawn carriages. Visitors to the castle are encouraged to talk to the workers. At Guédelon, you can peek into the past to see, hear, and experience what it may have been like to build a real castle from the ground up.

A LONG, SLOW PROCESS

When will Guédelon Castle be finished? Currently, the planners estimate that the project will finish up around 2030. Once completed, the castle will feature six turrets, a protective wall, bedrooms, a kitchen, a chapel, and more.

GILLETTE CASTLE STATE PARK

CONNECTICUT, UNITED STATES

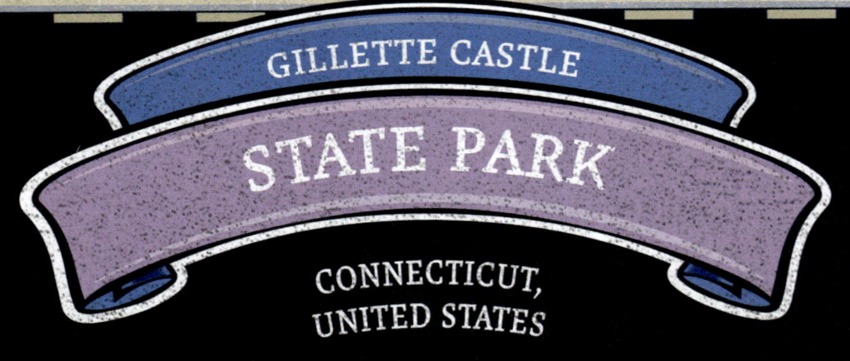

On a hill high above the Connecticut River, nestled in a wooded area, sits the 100-year-old Gillette Castle. This medieval-inspired mansion was built by William Gillette, an actor and playwright. Gillette personally designed the stone structure and lived in it from 1919 until his death in 1937.

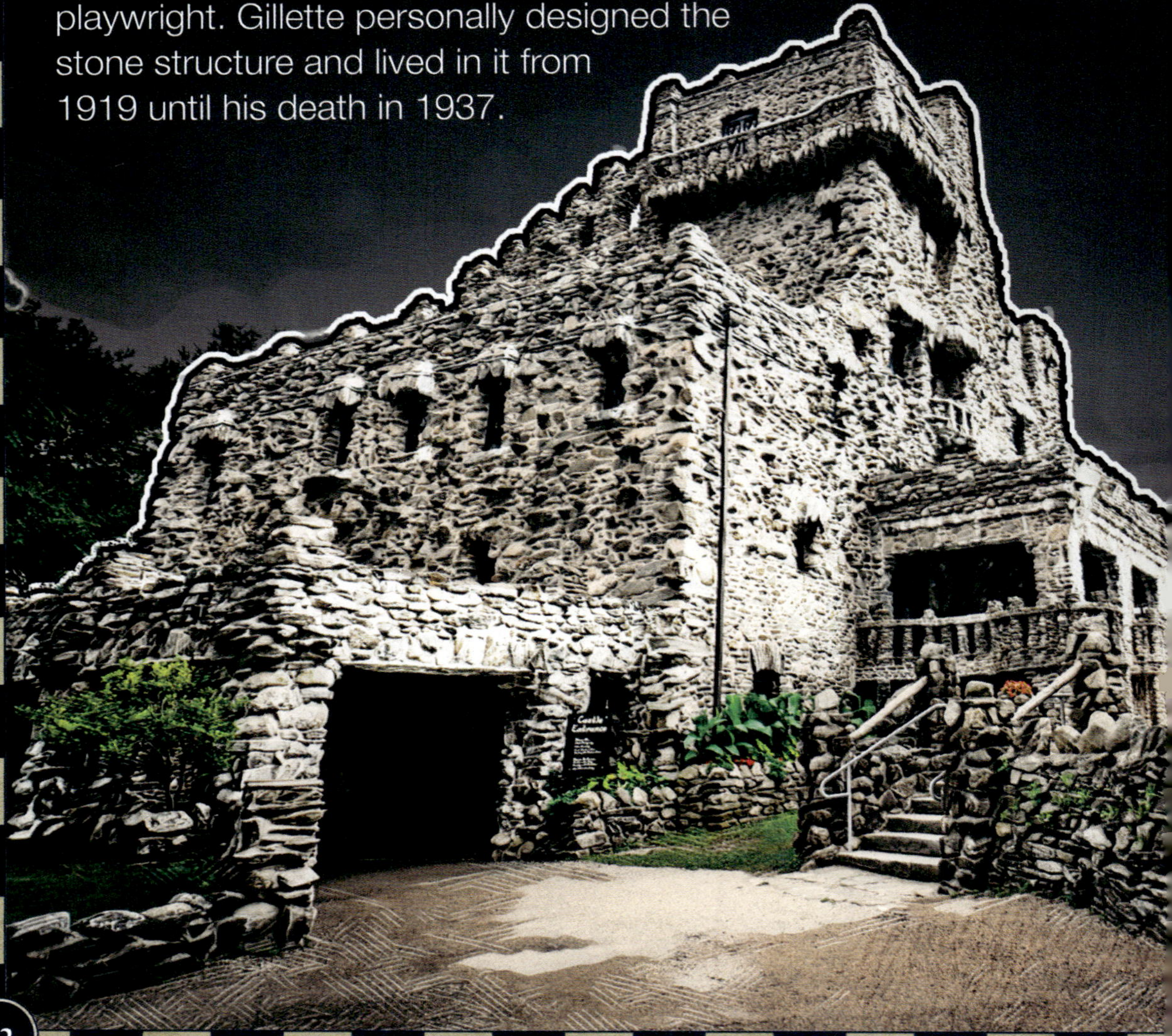

The castle was Gillette's dream house. It contains 24 unique rooms filled with secret nooks, built-in furniture, and hand-carved trick locks built into dozens of doors. In the Great Hall, Gillette installed mirrors that allowed him to spy on visitors. Around the property, Gillette built a three-mile miniature railway, countless trails, and even a goldfish pond.

As an actor, William Gillette's claim to fame was his portrayal of Sherlock Holmes.

KNOW BEFORE YOU GO

Want to visit real castles around the world? Before walking into one, you'll need to find out who owns it! Gillette is owned by the State of Connecticut. Other castles are owned by private families, governments, or non-profit organizations.

WE TRAVELED TO...

Find the location of each place you've traveled to while reading this book.

1. **Neuschwanstein Castle**: Schwangau, Germany

2. **Edinburgh Castle**: Edinburgh, Scotland

3. **Citadel of Aleppo**: Aleppo, Syria

4. **Great Zimbabwe**: Southeastern Zimbabwe

5. **Windsor Castle**: Windsor, England

6. **Himeji Castle**: Himeji, Japan

7. **Predjama Castle**: Predjama, Slovenia

8. **Qasr Kharana**: Amman, Jordan

9. **Maiden's Castle**: Kizklesi, Turkey

10. **Mont-Saint-Michel**: Normandy, France

11. **Pena Palace**: Sintra, Portugal

12. **Kelburn Castle**: North Ayrshire, Scotland

13. **Castle of Sammezzano**: Tuscany, Italy

14. **Alcázar of Segovia**: Segovia, Spain

15. **Chittorgarh**: Rajasthan, India

16. **Castillo de San Carlos de la Barra**: Zulia, Venezuela

17. **Kentucky Castle**: Kentucky, United States

18. **Guédelon Castle**: Treigny, France

19. **Gillette Castle State Park**: Connecticut, United States

GLOSSARY

abbey (AB-ee): a group of buildings, including a church, where monks or nuns live and work

archaeology (ahr-kee-AH-luh-jee): the study of the distant past, which often involves digging up old buildings, objects, and bones and examining them carefully

arrowslits (AR-oh-slits): narrow, vertical openings through which an archer can launch arrows

citadel (SI-tuh-del): a fortress that commands a city

colony (KAH-luh-nee): a territory that has been settled by people from another country and is controlled by that country

dungeon (DUHN-juhn): an underground prison

medieval (mee-DEE-vuhl): of or having to do with the Middle Ages, the period of history between approximately 1000 CE and 1450 CE

moat (moht): a deep, wide ditch dug around a castle, fort, or town and filled with water to prevent enemy attacks

monarchs (MAH-nurks): people who rule a country, such as kings or queens

pilgrimage (PIL-gruhm-udge): a journey to a holy place to worship there

residence (REZ-i-duhns): the place where someone lives; a home

turrets (TUR-itz): round or square towers on a building, usually on a corner

INDEX

TEXT-DEPENDENT QUESTIONS

1. What is the oldest and largest inhabited castle on Earth?

2. What makes Guédelon Castle so unique?

3. What purposes have castles served throughout history? List three.

4. Why does Shuri Castle have a red roof?

5. Why did some colonial leaders build castles?

EXTENSION ACTIVITY

Taking inspiration from the castles in this book, design your very own castle. Consider the following questions: Where will it be located? Will it have defensive features? Who will live there? What will it look like on the outside and the inside? Create a sketch, describe it in words, or build a model of your castle using craft supplies like clay or paper.

BIBLIOGRAPHY

Alnwick Castle, "Alnwick Castle Facts and Figures"
https://www.alnwickcastle.com/explore/the-history/facts-figures (accessed November 6, 2023).

Alnwick Castle, "Other Film and Television"
https://www.alnwickcastle.com/explore/on-screen/other-filming (accessed November 6, 2023).

American Press Institute, "Student Journalism Resources,"
https://www.americanpressinstitute.org/youth-news-literacy/resources/student-journalism-resources/,
(accessed January 9, 2019).

Architectural Digest, "World's most Instagrammable castle can be yours for $18.3M"
https://www.architecturaldigest.in/content/worlds-most-instagrammable-castle-tuscany-italy-18-million/
(accessed November 19, 2023).

Beardsley, Eleanor and Cristina Baussan. NPR. "In France, workers build a castle from scratch the
13th-century way." October 1, 2023.
https://www.npr.org/2023/10/01/1200546214/france-medieval guedelon-castle-burgundy
(accessed November 19, 2023).

Bran Castle, https://bran-castle.com/ (accessed November 6, 2023).

Britannica, The Editors of Encyclopaedia. "Bran Castle" https://www.britannica.com/topic/Bran-Castle (accessed
November 6, 2023).

Cruickshank, Dan. *Man-Made Wonders of the World.* London: Dorling Kindersley Limited, 2019. CT.gov,
"Gillette Castle State Park" https://portal.ct.gov/DEEP/State-Parks/Parks/Gillette-Castle-State-Park
(accessed November 19, 2023).

Hueneke, Erika. *The World's Most Amazing Castles: Timeless Treasures Around the Globe.* New York: Centennial
Books, 2020. Kelburn Estate, "Explore Kelburn"
https://www.kelburnestate.com/ (accessed November 19, 2023).

Museum With No Frontiers, "Discover Islamic Art"
https://islamicart.museumwnf.org/database_item.php?id=monument;ISL;jo;Mon01;25;en
(accessed November 8, 2023).

Royal Collection Trust, "Fact Sheet"
https://www.rct.uk/sites/default/files/Windsor_Castle_Fact_Sheet.pdf (accessed November 6, 2023).

Schloss Neuschwanstein, "Idea and History"
https://www.neuschwanstein.de/englisch/idea/index.htm (accessed November 7, 2023).

Scholastic Children's Dictionary. New York, NY: Scholastic, 2019.

Taylor, Alan. The Atlantic. "Building a 13th-Century Castle in the 21st Century."
https://www.theatlantic.com/photo/2016/09/building-a-13th-century-castle-in-the-21st-century/500204/
(accessed November 19, 2023).

UNESCO World Heritage Convention, "Ancient City of Aleppo"
https://whc.unesco.org/en/list/21/ (accessed November 7, 2023).

World Monuments Fund, "Citadel of Aleppo"
https://www.wmf.org/project/citadel-aleppo (accessed November 7, 2023).

Kaitlyn Duling is a reader, writer, and editor who grew up in Illinois. She now lives in Boston, Massachusetts, with her wife. When she isn't working with words, Kaitlyn loves to run marathons and travel the world. She hopes to one day visit many of the castles featured in this book! She has written more than 100 books for children and teens.

PHOTO CREDITS ©: Cover: MrsWilkins / Getty Images; Cover: Hailey Scragg; Cover: fogcatcher / Shutterstock.com; Cover: YOH YOH's VISUAL QUEST / Shutterstock.com; Cover: THANACHAI SRISAI / Shutterstock.com; Cover: Tatiana Popova / Shutterstock.com; Cover: Cavit Gencturk / Shutterstock.com; Page 1: ricorico / Getty Images; Page 1: Marti Bug Catcher / Shutterstock.com; Page 3: MrsWilkins / Getty Images; Page 4: gregobagel / Getty Images; Page 5: RudyBalasko / Getty Images; Page 5: Lodapon Wantaarawaiva / Shutterstock.com; Page 5: Aleh Varanishcha/ Getty Images; Page 6: Andrew Mayovskyy / Shutterstock.com; Page 7: COLUMBIA PICTURES / Album/Newscom; Page 7: Konstantin Yolshin / Shutterstock.com; Page 7: Natali Strelnik / Shutterstock.com; Page 8: lapas77 / Shutterstock.com; Page 8: Arcady / Shutterstock.com; Page 9: Wallophoto / Shutterstock.com; Page 10: Fly_and_Dive / Shutterstock.com; Page 11: Waj / Shutterstock.com; Page 12: DPST/Newscom; Page 12: Albert Junior mhaka / Getty Images; Page 14: Alexey Fedorenko / Shutterstock.com; Page 15: Sergii Figurnyi / Shutterstock.com; Page 15: Cherry Dale/Mirrorpix/Newscom; Page 16: Pond Thananat / Shutterstock.com; Page 17: Wunlop_Worldpix_Exposure / Shutterstock.com; Page 19: Janez Zalaznik / Shutterstock.com; Page 19: Mantonature / Getty Images; Page 19: Panama7 / Getty Images; Page 20: adaask / Getty Images; Page 20: Nataliya Nazarova / Shutterstock.com; Page 21: Dmitry Chulov / Shutterstock.com; Page 21: MIGUEL G. SAAVEDRA / Shutterstock.com; Page 21: nikolpetr / Shutterstock.com; Page 22: Cherry Dale /Mirrorpix/Newscom; Page 22: DPST/Newscom; Page 22: Rudmer Zwerver / Shutterstock.com; Page 23: Mazur Travel / Shutterstock.com; Page 24: Tjibbe Kampstra / Shutterstock.com; Page 24: Wwyloeck / Shutterstock.com; Page 25: wjarek / Shutterstock.com; Page 25: Beneda Miroslav / Shutterstock.com; Page 26: Serenity-H / Shutterstock.com; Page 27: yevtushenko serhii / Shutterstock.com; Page 27: torasun / Shutterstock.com; Page 28: K. Briehl/picture alliance / blickwinkel/K/Newscom; Page 29: K. Briehl/picture alliance / blickwinkel/K/Newscom; Page 29: K. Briehl/picture alliance / blickwinkel/K/Newscom; Page 29: Boris Stroujko / Shutterstock.com; pixel creator / Shutterstock.com; Page 30: RiumaLab / Shutterstock.com; Page 30: Reflex Life / Shutterstock.com; Page 30: pixel creator / Shutterstock.com; Page 32: Visual Intermezzo / Shutterstock.com; Page 32: Aleksandar Todorovic / Shutterstock.com; Page 32: trabantos / Shutterstock.com; Page 33: photomaster / Shutterstock.com; Page 34: Matyas Rehak / Shutterstock.com; Page 34: Igor Plotnikov / Shutterstock.com; Page 35: mrinalpal / Shutterstock.com; Page 36: Paperkites / Getty Images; Page 36: Wilfredor / Public Domain; Page 36: ksevgi / Shutterstock.com; Page 36: Sk_Advance studio / Shutterstock.com; Page 36: Carlos Amarillo / Shutterstock.com; Page 37: Diego Grandi / Shutterstock.com; Page 37: Andrei Medvedev / Shutterstock.com; Page 38: Mimi Foley / Shutterstock.com; Page 39: Paul Brady Photography / Shutterstock.com; Page 40: Rrrainbo / Getty Images; Page 40: AUFORT JEROME / Getty Images; Page 41: Carlos Perez Lopez / Getty Images; Page 41: Francois BOIZOT / Shutterstock.com; Page 42: Alexander Prokopenko / Shutterstock.com; Page 43: Yingna Cai / Shutterstock.com; Page 43: Halfpoint / Getty Images; Page 43: 4x6 / Getty Images; Page 43: Cynthia Liang / Shutterstock.com; Various pages: LoudRedCreative / Getty Images; Various pages: Anna Timoshenko/ Shutterstock.com; Various pages: Miodrag Kitanovic / Getty Images; Various pages: Andrey_Kuzmin / Shutterstock.com

Library of Congress PCN Data

Real Castles around the World / Kaitlyn Duling

(Travel to...)

ISBN 978-1-73165-803-6 (hard cover)
ISBN 978-1-73165-809-8 (soft cover)
ISBN 978-1-73165-815-9 (e-book)
ISBN 978-1-73165-821-0 (e-pub)
Library of Congress Control Number: 2024932712

Rourke Educational Media
Printed in the United States of America
03-0902511937

Edited by: **Hailey Scragg**
Cover and interior design/illustration by: **Joshua Janes**